JESUS, WHO HE IS

Unbelievably
amazing

JESUS, WHO HE IS

Unbelievably
amazing

CRACK TO CONVICT - CHRIST TO COLLEGE

SIDNEY H. SMITH III

JESUS, WHO HE IS UNBELIEVABLY AMAZING

Copyright © 2021 by Sidney H. Smith III. All rights reserved.

No part of this publication may be reproduced, stored in a retrieval system or transmitted in any way by any means, electronic, mechanical, photocopy, recording or otherwise without the prior permission of the author except as provided by USA copyright law.

This Book is dedicated to
my wife Judy.

Special Thanks to the many people GOD sent my way...Mama, Tyre B. Mills Jr., Sister Kathleen Spurlin, Sister Patricia (Pat) Garrison, Danny Pierce, Alvin Moody, Pastor Anthony McCullom, David Dilmore, Pastor Bryan Wilson, Pastor Downs, Pastor Josh Daniels, Pastor Atwood, Aunt Joyce, Jean Allgood, Christine Skinner, Pastor Adolph, Dr. Virginia Adolph, Leanne & Cliff Burris, Kairos (on the inside), Home of Grace, The Bradfords, Chief Papania, Nica Cason, Terry & Robert Cavert, Ken Covington, Dr. Nyugen CSWE, Derrith, Dr. Drumm, Paul Pyles MD, Wayne Elias, Grace Fisher (MDOC), Butch Oustalet, Vicky Murdy, Dr.WendyAnn Wyatt, Estelle (Will) Nail, Lisa Crain-Kersanac, Robert Graham, Kim Hanson, Perry & Glenda Ladner, Professor Karen Aderer, Deloris (Diva) Williams, Dr. Kolbo, Cynthia Luna, Mercy House Teen Challenge, Ted & Mary Murphy, Pastor Susan Eaton, Jennifer Parks, H. Gordon Myrick, Chief Chris Read, Chief Chris Ryles, Lawrence & Lucimarian Roberts, Dr. Ronald E. McNair, Rep. Sonya Williams-Barnes, Dr. Tilly, Dr. Laquesta, Q & Shelbi,

CONTENTS

Introduction 9

Chapter 1: Growing Up 15

Chapter 2: The Miracle of Judy 27

Chapter 3: Pack It Up! 31

Chapter 4: God Ordered My Steps 40

Chapter 5: A New Life 53

Chapter 6: Moving Forward 82

Chapter 7: Recent Interviews 86

Chapter 8: My Many Blessings 95

Conclusion 103

INTRODUCTION

At the age of 42, after a lifetime of drug addiction, crime, and prison, I had a deeply moving life changing encounter with CHRIST. I had long believed myself to be a Christian, regardless of the drugs and crime. I believed in God and believed myself to have a "good heart" that God could see and understand. Despite my wrong-doing, I believed that I demonstrated faith by professing to be a believer and follower of Jesus. At times, I was able to put aside my wrong-doing and attempted to live a more Christian lifestyle. Most of these times were when I was in prison. I read the Bible, participated in church and choir, ministered to other inmates, and found ways to have compassion in a very negative environment. Again, I truly *thought* I was a Christian who had found salvation. Unfortunately, this was all apparently an exterior version of Christianity that didn't really translate into a true way of life.

After serving 10 straight years in prison, being released, returning to drug use, and crime after about a year and a half, I was at a crossroad. I found myself in the latest of a long list of addiction rehabilitation programs called Mercy House Adult & Teen Challenge. This came about, not because of any profound desire on my part to turn my life around, but because it was the only way I could avoid being sent back to prison. This was a 14-month residential program, entirely spiritual, Christian, and Bible-based. I was separated, once again, from my family; my wife, my mother, and my son, as I had been when I was incarcerated, on the street, and using drugs. There was no relevant issue involving family, other than the emotional stress, embarrassment, and worry that my behavior caused for all of us.

The Teen Challenge program is a very strict one, and I was just biding my time following the rules and doing as I was instructed to do, as any master manipulator would do that had spent 70% of his life living on the street. I had no thought that this program might be an answer for my disaster of a life or that God could or would care enough to change me. At that point in my life, I was sincerely hopeless. I was resigned to a life of being a crack addict. I did *try* to change, to stop doing drugs, in many of the previous rehabs I had entered, as well as in my normal everyday life. But it was always to no avail.

There would be periods of sobriety and focus on my spiritual well-being, but those times never lasted. After seven months of residence and participation in the Teen Challenge program, I was literally at my wits end. I was angry, miserable, and hopeless. During the middle of one day, I went into the room where I slept, which we were not allowed to do according to the rules of the program. I went there because I knew I could be alone. I felt such immense emotions boiling inside of me that I knew I was about to explode.

I didn't want anyone to see me cry or fall apart, so I went to my room. I closed the door and began to scream out loud to God. I said to Him: "If you are who they say you are, you need to fix my life for me because I can't do it!" I cried, I screamed, and let go of all the anger and pain I held in for so long. After this "conversation" with God, in which I unconsciously and totally surrendered myself to Him, everything changed for me. I didn't even really understand what was going on. I just knew I was different. I felt a spiritual connection that allowed me to feel freedom from addiction as well as feel compassion for others. Both things were totally new and unfamiliar to me. As I continued for another eight months to the completion of the program, my life took on new meaning. I was learning and growing in spiritual ways that allowed me to see the world, others and myself in a whole new and hopeful way.

Truly the spiritual experience I had with God had changed me and my life forever. The year was 2012, and there were not any societal issues that affected or influenced this spiritual event of mine. My life, however, had been transformed completely and continues to be to this day.

The greatest implication for other Christians and most especially, addicts, is that I know for certain now that no matter what the history or current situation, there is hope for change wi Christ. God made me a new creation. This provides me a great deal of faith to be able to deal with "impossible" situations. For me, Christ, is the very foundation of my ability to translate hope and healing to others through this book.

Amid my busy, now wonderful everyday activities, I saw *the* email notification on my phone. I could tell this was the email I had been waiting for the last few weeks. It seemed like it was going to be good news from the words I could see, but I was not going to open the email up without my wife Judy. She and I had been through everything together and I was not going to keep this to myself. Good news, great news, or even the bad, Judy and I were going to see this email together.

I ran into the room where Judy was, and I was almost crying. "Judy, I think this may be good news about my dream job, but I want us to open it together!"

Judy and I opened the email and said, "Sidney, this is the best news! You got the job you have been wanting!" We both cried and thanked GOD for answered prayers. What a difference Christ has made in my life and what a difference today has been from this same day just a few years ago. Today, I am just two weeks away from a new job at the VA working with Veterans as a licensed master social worker.

I have had experience digging in trash cans to survive and stealing to get enough money for my next fix. I cry when I think of the miracle that is my life. And now to think of where I am I cannot imagine anything else but gratitude. I always felt that people crossed my path at the right times. Although at those times I didn't always notice. Now, looking back I can see clearly. Those people were there planting seeds or watering seeds that had been previously planted by someone else.

My editor and I have gone back and forth about the title and subtitle of this book. I wanted From *Crack to Christ* and College to something. At first it was going to be Absolutely Amazing. And for some reason that stuck in my editor's head. So, when I came up with From *Crack to Christ*, she insisted the subtitle be *Amazing Grace*.

The more I thought about that subtitle the more I liked it. Because it has been grace from God that has brought me from where I was to where I am now. Amazing grace. I had seed planters all along the way, but until I was ready to accept the grace God was offering and make the choice God was offering to me, I was going to keep floundering on my own way. My wife titled the book Unbelievably Amazing. God has sent me so many people to intervene in my life. Seed Planters is what they were. Judy was a person who stayed and stuck through it all until I finally embraced the GOD who relentlessly pursued me. I was willing to see God for who HE was finally, after leaving no stone unturned searchig for a fix. This is HIS story of my life through the depths of darkness to HIS grace, which Unbelievably Amazing.

INTRODUCTION

Chapter 1

GROWING UP

A Long Look Back

I grew up in a poor neighborhood in Oakland. But unlike many, I never had to do without. I was born and raised in Oakland, California. Kaiser Permanente is the name of the hospital I was born in. I was born to Gloria Graham and Sidney Smith Jr. on February 18, 1970, are the month, day, and year, and I weighed 10 lbs. at birth. From birth to about 10 years old most memories are foggy and what you're reading in detail is from my mother. I do have lots of childhood pictures for evidence of places like Disneyland at the age of 2.

My biological father has never participated in any of my life. My entire childhood was spent basically under the pretense of a stepdad being the only father I knew. I didn't find out about who my father was until much later in life. It was then that I found out he lived in Chicago and left my mother and me when I was born. My mother then married my stepdad, Johnny Moore. One memory I have of him is a fishing trip. I don't recall a lot of information about the fishing trip other than lots of red snappers, and huge fish sporadically being put out on our front lawn taking pictures. I know the boat trip passed through the San Francisco Bay out into the Pacific Ocean from the

Golden Gate Bridge. He was involved with a very large percentage of my childhood ranging from 2 until 12. Mom said he almost left me and my mother when I was a baby.

I recall my mother in the kitchen cooking and something smelling good. I was just a kid, under 10 years old, and entered the kitchen with excitement about something smelling good. I ended up burning the roof of my mouth with caramel. My mother told me to blow it and let it cool down, but I just could not wait to put that caramel into my mouth. Yell, I did.

Travel

I had a great childhood. Growing up in Oakland California was wild and crazy, but good. As a child, my mother was my sole provider as she worked for the United States Postal Service in West Oakland. When I was a child, my mother was married to my stepdad. He was not there for me as a father growing up. My mother raised me with the help of our next-door neighbor and other babysitters while she worked. I remember traveling across the country from California to Mississippi in a camper. We stopped and vacationed in places such as Santa Fe, New Mexico. I remember us stopping in the Mojave Desert and the flies were bad. I mean we practically were held hostage in the camper by heat and flies. It was an unforgettable moment. My mom and stepdad took us everywhere. We traveled to baseball games and ate hot dogs, with our gloves hoping to catch a foul ball.

As a child, our family had a vacation spot called Clear Lake, in Clear Lake California. We also traveled to Napa Valley wine country, Sonoma Valley, Redwood trees, Lake Tahoe, and a host of other cities, states, and events. These trips and travel as a young kid were not all fun for me, but some chips were motivational in discipline and work ethic. I remember going to San Fernando Valley to pick Black Eyed Peas, Okra, Purple Hull Peas, Corn, and Green Beans. I also very clearly remember shelling peas for weeks, so we could put them in the freezer. I also remember the green beans and snapping them into pieces and pulling the ends off and freezing them. As a kid, I didn't enjoy making my thumbs sore as a result of shelling peas for hours and hours, day after day.

Music

I started piano at the age of 5 years old. I specifically remember this moment. Mother asked me, "What do you want to do?" I told her that I wanted to play the piano. She said, "OK." and the next thing I knew, we had a piano delivered to our home. It was a Kimball upright and we still have it. At the age of 5 years old I started having private piano lessons. My instructor was a classical pianist and taught all types of music. I grew up playing classical, boogie, pop, rock, and a little jazz.

My music lessons lasted about 7 years until my instructor died. Every year we had 2 major piano performances. One performance was an audition with a judge and 10 memorized pieces. The other performance was a recital and as a class, we played the same 10 pieces. The concertos and sonatas were ten pages or more!

I picked up Stevie Wonder as my idol and owned all of his albums. I tried learning his music and I could play a few of his songs. They were all very tough. He is a genius. I remember reading the back of his songs in the *Key of Life* album where it says Produced, Written, Arranged, and Performed by Stevie Wonder. In another place on the album, it read "All instruments played by Stevie Wonder". I repeat, he is a genius. I joined his fan club and saw his "Hotter than July Tour". On the night of his concert in Oakland, California, John Lennon was killed in New York. During the concert Stevie Wonder was escorted off stage, I mean in the middle of the concert. Stevie Wonder was approached by someone and they whispered in his ear and he just stopped playing and got up and walked off stage leaving the entire coliseum shocked. After returning 10 to 20 minutes later, he was crying and told us all what had just happened to John Lennon.

Concerts

When I was a child growing up my mother took me to lots of concerts. Seeing Stevie Wonder is most likely my favorite and most memorable. Stevie Wonder was who I looked up to as a child musician. Other stars that I was blessed to see as a kid included Michael Jackson, Marvin Gaye, B. B. King, and Maze featuring Frankie Beverly, Aretha Franklin, and The O'Jays, The list of various concerts goes on and on.

Our concert with Michael Jackson was somewhat of an adventure. As a child, my family had a huge camper that we used for travel. One afternoon mother said we all would go out to dinner. We got into the motor home to go out to dinner which I thought was strange. But as a kid I quickly let it go and began focusing on something else. We did go out to eat at one of our favorite places in San Francisco called Victorian Station. After dinner was concluded we traveled back to Oakland across the Bay Bridge onto the Nimitz Freeway. The motorhome ended up in the parking lot at the Oakland Coliseum. The Oakland Area where the Oakland A's, Oakland Raiders and Golden State Warriors play. I knew there was something weird going on, I remember thinking that the motor home was broken and had a problem. We parked and went into the Coliseum and to my surprise Michael Jackson and the Jackson 5 came out on the stage. I turned to look at my mother with amazement and still to this day those exact emotions flood my heart and mind. I was overwhelmed with joy and tears and the crowd all stood to their feet yelling at the top of their lungs. That was one night I'll never forget thanks to my Mom.

As a kid, football and basketball were not my things. I recall trying out for peewee football several years in a row. During those years of try-outs, I also recall not making the team each year. I will say that most of the reason for me not making the team is due to weight. I was a fat kid and I could not make the weight list for the teams that I tried out for each year. Basketball was kind of the same thing where

I tried to play and never made the team. The only difference with basketball was there was no weight clause. However, I just didn't have the skill to compete with the other kids my age.

I liked baseball a lot as a kid. I remember playing little league baseball. My coach was a nurse who volunteered his time to coach a bunch of neighborhood kids. His name was Coach Valentine. I was taught to play catcher, left field, and second base. My favorite and best position was behind the plate as a catcher. I mostly remember batting in the clean-up position, number four. I can't recall any stats or anything like that, but I was pretty good at it.

Other Cultures

My mother was the greatest cook ever. As a child, I ate homemade potato chips, doughnuts, and gumbo. Mom and step-dad had a catering business and hosted very large events.

My mother made sure I grew up with knowledge and taste from many cultures. As a family, we had several favorite restaurants. San Francisco, California, was where we frequented Chinatown and an authentic restaurant named Yet Wah on Pier 39. The waiter and waitresses were all Chinese. As a child, I remember the ladies had chopsticks in their hair. Hot tea was brought to the table. The small delicate teacups had Chinese writing on them. Pot Stickers and a dish named Sub Gum Yee Won Ton was my personal favorite. My mom insisted that I learn to eat with chopsticks, and I did. Soon we had chopsticks at home and I was using them there. Thanks again to my Mom!

One Childhood Glitch

I am not completely sure what triggered this event. I was feeling disconnected from my mom at this time. I think it was about the time my stepdad left. At age twelve I took a whole bottle of pills. I perceived my mom's love and attention were just not there. I always received the physical things I needed, but there was a distance. I remember I'd go to any extreme I could to get her attention. Finally, I just downed the whole bottle. I was desperate for any sign that she cared. The next thing I knew I was having my stomach pumped. From the hospital, I remember going to an institution and she left me there. It broke my heart.

Education

I did well in school from kindergarten on up until I dropped out. Ms. Terry was my Kindergarten teacher and I remember her being very nice to me. My first year of kindergarten was spent in the public school system in a school named Whittier Elementary in the heart of East Oakland. I lose sight of memories from first, second, and third grades. I can't remember where I spent those years.

I do recall the name of the next school I attended. It was Eastmont Christian Academy. This school was a private Christian K-12 School. We had to memorize scripture and I remember starting with the book of Genesis. As a result of scripture memory, I do remember memorizing the entire first chapter of the book of Genesis. The school founder and director Dr. William H. Coleman Jr. became somewhat of a mentor of mine.

One memory that I have about that school is that my Mom insisted that I walk to school a different route other than the shortest. All the kids from my neighborhood went to a public school up the street called Frick Junior High. My mom knew there was a lot of fighting going on all the time on the shortest route. So, smiling as I write this, I remember as a kid walking to school one day and being disobedient by taking the shortest route instead of the way she suggested. She then met me at the end of the route to catch me red-handed.

St. Cyril's Catholic is another school I went to and there are two distinct memories I have about my time there. One is having an injury by hitting my head on a basketball pole and my mother left her job to come to see me. The other memory involves a science project that a classmate and I made. The project was a movie we created by drawing scenes on a long sheet of paper. The paper was rolled up on 2 sticks and put into a box that had a hole cut out of it for viewing. I remember my classmate and I became really good friends. His name was Phong and he was Vietnamese.

The Beginning of my Down Time

The very first time I remember using drugs was in the ninth grade. I transferred from a Catholic school named Saint Mary's College High School into the public school system. The name of the school that I transferred into was named Emeryville High located in Emeryville, California. My mother, I had recently relocated from Oakland to Emeryville during divorce proceedings from my step-dad. I was in Mississippi at the time of the filing for divorce and came home to a small one-bedroom apartment with my mother. This is the time in my life a lot went wrong. The neighbors that lived in the apartment next door were drug addicts and the people who lived up front were also drug addicts.

The neighbors next door and out front were both adults with families and I was just a child in the ninth grade in high school. Of course, I had dabbled into weed and alcohol and some other miscellaneous drugs but wasn't addicted to any at that time. However, when I moved into that 1-bedroom apartment with my mother in Emeryville and those neighbors so close by, I soon became addicted to using and dealing. I started trying to sell the drugs at school. It was only weed, and I wanted to be popular so it was what I did.

One of the things I remember most about my thought process was wanting to be accepted, liked, and fit in. There were only 2 drug dealers at the school who were the weed men for everybody in the entire school. It was me and another guy. We became friends or at least I thought we were. We both had a private group of customers and sometimes we would fade each other by smoking joints from our stash with each other. Most days we would spend our lunch period out on the football field in the bleachers after getting two Old English 40 ounces where we would drink and fade each other's joints.

This went on for quite a while and a distinct memory then I had was my birthday. On this day the other guy knew it was my birthday and he wanted to supply all the weed we smoked that day. There was something different about the weed that day, I felt different. Not only did I feel different, but I also smelled a different sweet smell, a new taste, and a laid-back mellow high. This felt weird at first, but the feelings quickly settled, and I liked the way that I was feeling. When I looked at my so-called friend, passing and smoking the same joint with me to ask him where he got this weed and where I could get some, he said he had my back.

Crack cocaine laced in weed had become, what I thought at that moment, a new friend, was my nemesis. It was a slow progression of cocaine use at first and appeared to be under control. The need to use crack cocaine placed in weed grew exponentially over the next few weeks and months. Before I knew it, I'd lost my job, my grades were suffering, and my relationship with my mother turned very negative, very fast.

As a Young Adult in California

I remember moments with guns pointed at my head, in a place and position where if I was killed nobody would have found me or known I was missing for months. I can likewise remember other times when I was so hungry, digging in garbage dumpsters for food and underneath my breath would be uttering a prayer for anything to eat. There were these Christians who would approach me offering food, shelter, and a shower. It was usually not in that order. Most of the time they wanted me to take a shower first. God would send these people at the perfect time. I would always be drugged out, hungry, and my body close to shutting down due to a lack of sleep. This is what happens when an addict like me doesn't eat or sleep for days. The only thing I had done was stay high. I was finally crashing, and my body needed food, water, and sleep or I would fall out by those dumpsters I was digging in.

In fact, after eating I would literally fall asleep and stay asleep for days. I spent a few seconds thinking occasionally, about those Christian people. Why on earth would they keep coming back to me to offer a place to shower, more food, a change of clothes, and a place to live? They knew I was a junkie. They had to know. They found me on the street every week stinking, dirty, half-clothed, and talking to myself. I was always high on drugs and aimlessly wandering around uptown Berkeley or digging in my favorite dumpsters. They knew who I was and didn't care, because if I stayed on that corner, in that area, they came as if they were looking for me. If I were completely honest, I thought those people were crazy, a cult, or just out of their minds, because I thought of myself as a terrible person, and they had to know. Everyone else did and wanted nothing to do with me unless they were drug addicts and also on the street.

My being on the street living homeless was not a bad deal, or so I thought at the time. I blended in with hundreds of other people living on the streets. In the city of Berkeley, California, there is a park by the name of People's Park. The park was full of people 24 hours a day. Most of the people were set up in tents, others had cars, and still, some had Volkswagen vans. Day and night, people were camping out, playing music, smoking weed, shooting heroin, tripping off acid pills, and drinking. Acid and pills had a lot to do with the scene as well. I'm still not sure, but I'm thinking these folks were called deadheads, hippies, or something of the like. It was white folks with French braids, dreadlocks, and purple, blue and red hair. These people also dressed very conservatively with lots of hardware like body piercing, earrings, and costume jewelry. There were Nazis with spiked hair and white supremacist too. I fit in well due to a common theme. We all wanted to get high and stay high.

My life during this period consisted of peddling weed off to support my crack habit. I tried other drugs but always preferred crack cocaine. As an addict living on the street, my primary concern 24 hours a day was getting high, how I was going to get high, and when I ran out of dope how I was going to get more. I lived on the street behind a coffee shop and restaurants directly across the street from People's Park. I kept a larger cardboard box to sleep on. I had it hidden and pushed between a fence and a garbage dumpster. What I remember most about that time is the drive to stay high. My motivation to stay high on crack trumped freedom, hygiene, eating, shelter, health, and life itself.

I would run my body for days, 24 hours a day, chasing the drug with no food, water, or rest. Eventually, my body would naturally begin to shut down and it was then that I would stop drug behavior and seek food. My food sources on the street consisted of selecting garbage dumpsters on certain days from behind different restaurants. I have no clue how I came up with the science behind this behavior.

I only remember doing it like clockwork. Local restaurants had different days of the week that bread would be thrown out. This bread would be old, with most of it had a bite taken out of it already as if it were part of someone's dinner that they didn't finish.

The bread was probably thrown in the trash by the busboy. Eventually, the trash from that restaurant would end up in the dumpster outside where I would dig through and find food. I easily recall a mental play-by-play flipping the dumpster back and grabbing a bag. Before tearing the bag open, I would always feel the corners of the bag for liquid. If the bag had liquid in it, it meant that the busboy or kitchen crew threw sodas, ice, and water out in the garbage bag with the half-eaten food. Liquid in the bag meant soggy bread and I didn't want any of that.

So, I developed the science of digging in the dumpsters for food only, not liquid. I kept repeating the sequence of discovery. If the corners did not yield the feeling of water, I would open the bags and search for partially eaten bread and leftover parts of meals.

The area had one coffee and pastry shop that would give me old donuts every week instead of throwing them in the trash. I remember walking into that donut shop for the first time like it happened yesterday. I was hungry, dirty, stinking, and tired. I'd been up for days chasing dope and my body was crashing and shutting down. I walked into the donut shop at closing and just begged for food. The shop worker gave me a cardboard box of old pastries, muffins, and scones. I had no sense of pride.

People stared at me as if I was an animal all day everywhere I went. I assumed that just desensitized me so I could walk around them and not care what they thought or said. I sat out in front of restaurants on weekend nights positioning myself close to the door where every patron entering and exiting heard my voice begging for change and/or food. I am talking about a bum. I was stinky, half-clothed, dirty, and a drug addict on the street harassing people. The restaurants rarely asked me to leave because my behavior was sadly normal among the many people in that area that did the same things night and day.

And of course, there were those days that I had hit a good payday stealing or conning someone out of money and bought myself food. I always bought something cheap because I had to have enough left for my fix. Even in those days, I distinctly remember putting crack first and more important than eating. Meaning I would settle and buy just enough to get by and always made sure I had the exact money needed for the drug deal to go the way I wanted it to.

My crimes during this time included stealing to support a drug habit. The University of California at Berkeley's uptown area near Blonde's Pizza was jumping with parties every weekend. Fraternity Houses were filled with drunken students, loud music, and victims of my crack addiction. I would weasel my way in somehow, sometimes right through the front door, and walk around scoping the place, stinking, half clothed, and dirty as if I belonged there. Other times I would arrive early in the morning, maybe 3:00 or 4:00am, and everybody would be passed out and I would walk through stepping over sleeping bodies to get into purses or pickup wallets that were easily accessible.

I remember times walking through these frat houses and opening room doors to people having sex and they would yell for me to exit as if I were just another college student accidentally going into the wrong room. I always carried a backpack and would leave with college books, CDs, jewelry, money, and anything else I thought had value. I knew from the experience of stealing and selling the items what type of books the college bookstores would pay the most for when you sold them back. I also was selective about the CDs I stole because I knew the type of CDs the music store would purchase from me for the highest prices.

Numerous attempts at rehab failed, and by the time I left for Mississippi at age twenty-three, I was an addict running from police and desperately hoping for a new start.

> Romans 15:5
>
> *"May the God who gives endurance and encouragement give you the same attitude of mind toward each other that Christ Jesus had."*

Chapter 2

THE MIRACLE OF JUDY

Judy's View of Me

"I remember him coming in," as Judy reminisced. "He'd been out on the streets for days, and the bottoms of his feet were just like hamburger meat because he had just been walking and walking and searching to do drugs." We were still newlyweds. I had known he had occasional bouts with drugs, but this was a sign of a full-blown addiction.

How do I describe love and life with an addict? I don't know if it's possible…especially if it's not something that you have experienced. It's a living hell on earth. It's watching someone you love slowly but surely killing themselves. It's never knowing when or where you may see them again, after being absent from home for days or weeks at a time. It's dreading hearing the phone ring because it might be 'that' call from the police or a hospital. It's suffocating! It's painful and terrifying. It's love and fear and hate all at the same time. It's frustrating and all-consuming.

JESUS, WHO HE IS—UNBELIEVABLY AMAZING

Judy summed up her former life when I was on drugs. There was nothing 'normal' about day-to-day life. No one understood in those moments why she still cared. Most said, "WHY do you care when you've been hurt over and over?" These are just some of the things that go with living with an addict. I know because I lived with all these things…and more! The addict in my life was my husband. I loved him, but there were moments in time when I simultaneously hated him or certainly hated what he was doing to himself and me. What do I do? Where do I turn? There were so many excellent, endearing qualities to this man who was being held hostage by a savage drug. There were skills, abilities, and talents…and yes, potential. Those are the things that kept me hanging on. Things that I believe God allowed me to see when no one else could.

Judy's voice was the voice of God through her. Her love was a holy abiding love that she was only able to give me because God loved her first. Her love was and is so special. I will never take it for granted again.

Judy believed that in all the years of crime, infidelity, rehabs, street life, prison, and only infrequent times of living at home, actually having a job, and being present that I could just not help what I was doing. She believed there are not very many things that she knew for absolute certainty, but one was that I wanted to stop doing drugs, wanted a sober life, and did everything I could to make that happen.

Judy believed I was just unable to do so, at least for any consistent length of time. There were "moments" – some good "moments." But that's all they were – "moments." In Judy's own words, "Those moments gave me a glimmer of hope. God was showing me the possibilities that I needed desperately to believe in. And I did! "For I can do everything through Christ, who gives me strength." Philippians 4:13 NLT

I would imagine all this description has painted a very bleak picture so far…but wait. The best is yet to come. You will probably find the best to be unbelievably amazing, and that's not an exaggeration or hyperbole. What is it? It's God's grace and mercy, as well as a lot of time, hard work, and effort to follow His lead. "He just turned around and looked at me, again, with tears in his eyes and just said, "I'm not going to make it; am I? I knew in my mind that I wasn't going to ever quit, because I had tried," said Sidney.

Judy and I met at a job interview in 1993 in Gulfport, Mississippi. I was coming from Oakland, California, and was hoping for a new start. Judy was the hiring manager. Judy said, "He had a real leadership ability about him because he just sort of would take charge of something once, he was given a task to do."

So, Judy not only hired me, but she also fell in love with me. And I did her, as much as I could love someone at that time. We were married less than one year later. You think you know people, but you don't know people really until you live with someone. I had told her about my addiction, but not the extent of my addiction. In fact, I was able to hide the depth of my addiction. After a few months of marriage, the truth began to spill out. Judy, believing that love and hope would prevail, saw Sidney through God's eyes, and continued to be hurt over and over again. And still, she hung on.

Judy believed in me. Her hope in me gave me some direction to some faith that God was drawing me into this for a reason. Keeping hope alive was another matter. Arrested in 1996 on outstanding warrants, Sidney would spend 13 years behind bars, and despite finding religion in prison, he relapsed soon after his release.

I still felt like something was missing. Like my salvation just did not take or something. I just didn't have what I needed inside of me. Nothing satisfied the hole. It was like a bottomless pit. Disappearing at times for weeks, I would bounce between bouts of sobriety and addiction.

"There were points in time for me when I was desperately sad, afraid, angry, resentful. I went through all those things, but it would always come back full circle to have the hope," said Judy, "This was the part of him that I had always loved; the joyful, kind, compassionate, loving person. He was so willing to do whatever it took. And again, I guess that's just the God, the hope, and the faith in me that just believed."

> Jeremiah 17:14
>
> *Heal me, Lord, and I will be healed; save me and I will be saved, for you are the one I praise.*

Chapter 3

PACK IT UP!

I do not talk about my prison life very much but just to give you some background so you can get the feel for how important my release day was to me when it did happen. Inmates start their day very early in the morning. Some places are set to begin at 4:30 am and some at 5:00 am. The day begins early. Breakfast is served right away so if you are late, you may not eat food again for another twelve to fourteen hours, depending on when evening chow is.

Right after breakfast, the inmate count begins, and you had better pray that count is right. Depending on the size of the prison, this can last almost an hour. After the count, the work "detail" begins. If you work in the kitchen you must get up around 2 am or 3 am to prepare the morning meal.

I will share one story that is cute and shows what a big heart my son has. In a way, this story is sad when I think back to that day. I saw my little boy as an inmate in prison. Visitation is a huge event. Prison has two major events, mail, and visitation. These are the two main events of the population where I was housed because not many people were going home. My living quarters housed mostly lifers and life without the possibility of parole. Visitation was on Saturdays for the building I lived in for more than 8 years. My wife was a regular visitor every two weeks.

Before being sentenced to prison I had a son. He was maybe 2 years old when I started my 20-year sentence. My son's mother vowed that I would never see him again. I had only seen him twice from birth to two years old, so hearing that I would never see him hadn't affected me. I had no idea how to be a father, a man, or a decent human being.

After being in prison for more than 5 years I got a request to add him and his mother to my visitation list. To my surprise, my son and his mother came to visit. So, I hear my name called for visitation and I begin the journey to the visitation building. All kinds of stuff were running through my mind about what to say, what to expect, and how to act. I had no idea of what being a dad entailed. Before entering the visitation room area each inmate enters into an adjacent room to be searched.

Nothing can go out with you into the visitation area. As I'm standing in line to be searched, I can see people going to and from the vending machines through a narrow opening in the door. Then, out of nowhere, he walks right up to the window and looks directly at me. There are several other inmates in the line ahead of me waiting to be searched. This kid locks his eyes on me. Remember now, I had only seen my son one time, and then he was just an infant. I'll never forget that moment when he walked up to the opening in the door and just locked eyes with me. It was as if I had a fire burning in my heart while that was happening. He eventually walked away, and I was searched and allowed into the visitation area.

Upon entering the visitation room, I scanned with my eyes to find my family. I saw my mother, in her wheelchair, my dad, my son, and his mother all sitting together. I approached them and began my visit. Not long after sitting down, I noticed my son had a bag of quarters in his hand. My mother had also brought quarters. The quarters are for the vending machines filled with snacks, candies, and drinks. I invited my son to go with me to the vending machines for food. He said ok, and off we went to the vending machines. He still had the quarters wrapped tightly around his hand, so I assumed that we would just use those. Once we arrived at the vending machine and made choices about the selections, I asked him for the quarters to insert into the machine.

He withdrew his hand and shook his head back and forth as if to say no. My first thought was that he was saving money and that his mother and my mother were responsible for instilling this behavior pattern into his mind. I said nothing else and retreated to the table where my mother had a bag of quarters. After obtaining the other bag of quarters, we walked back to the vending machines. The visit continued, we ate, laughed, and got to know each other.

Hours later the officer at the desk in the front of the room stood and yelled "Visitation is now over, offenders to the back." My son began to look around the room as people began standing and hugging each other saying their goodbyes. I could see the panic on his face. I was standing and his mother was calling him to come around to her side of the table. My son refused her orders and his mother was now on her way around the table to get him. I remember feeling his tiny hand squeezing my pants. As his mother approached, she reached out and grabbed his free hand. As she pulled him away and I felt his hand give way, he snatched his hand free from her grip and ran towards the front of the room.

I started after him and so did his mother. Before either of us could get to him he was at the guard's desk and had thrown the sack of quarters into the air. I stopped. quarters were all over the desk and floor as the guard was making her way around to my son. I heard him say, "Bail my daddy out of jail." He was saving the quarters intending to bring me home with him…

Nights in prisons are unpredictable. That is the least supervised time of the day. Prison life can be dangerous if you become a target. You have to always be watching. When you spend years behind bars you are keeping yourself at a hyper-vigilant state; it becomes a situation where some former inmates find they have PTSD upon release and also have a difficult time sleeping years after release.

Prisons for profit are the worst. They have very little regard for how many people they cram into their facilities. Most violence happens in prisons for profit. Once a prisoner gets released, they are faced with a life of a record, unable to vote, and difficult job prospects because they do have a record.

I know I have been blessed and favored by the LORD. Judy and I have worked hard seeing adversity as opportunities since graduating from Mercy House Teen Challenge. Please know, it is hard work from a high school dropout to a Masters degree and to see life dreams come true. I could not have done any of those things without the support of Judy or the direction from God. I had to stay with it. Drug addicts are used to getting instant gratification. Working for a degree takes a long time. You have to train yourself to accept the little victories. The big goal does not come right away. Going for a degree is not an instant "high." But in the long run, it sure is worth it! Thank you Jesus!

Now that I've shared a little bit of what prison life can be, I want to share the amazing feeling upon hearing these words, "Pack it up!"

Pack It Up!

Lying in bed, eyes wide open. People are beginning to wake up and move about around me. I see people traveling back and forth going back to their beds and the bathroom area. Lighting in the building is still very dim and low. It is almost breakfast time. I can tell by the faint light from the sun rising providing additional light through the broken windows in the building.

"T 8 1 6 4 pack it up" is announced over the intercom without warning. That is the announcement that has kept me awake all night long. I've waited literally an entire decade for that particular announcement. I raised, sliding my feet to the floor, and men from all over the building were coming towards me. Men were reaching out their hands to shake mine in congratulatory fashion.

The entire building was up, alive, and moving about with excitement. You see, just the fact of one man being called for release to go home was an injection of hope to the entire prison. Some men knew they would never leave alive and still were happy to see me go. I floated off the rack (bed) to my feet, stuff already packed and lying next to me on the floor. I began greeting the men who had presented themselves to say their last goodbyes to me. We shook hands and hugged, others presented torn pieces of paper with their Department of Corrections number and name on it for me to write. Most men just stood at the end of their racks savoring every move I made as if to create a movie in their minds as if they were me and I was them.

I grabbed the knotted sheet which was tied at the top with all the personal belongings I owned and wanted to keep. It was very light because in anticipation of this event I'd given most of what I owned to those closest to me the night before. In my sheet, I carried the most prized possessions an inmate could call his own. The sheet contained letters, cards, and pictures accumulated over 10 years from my wife.

I headed towards the front of the building, and it appeared the entire building was up to see me out. As I approached the metal door I could see through the glass to the other building. What I saw in the other building was men crowding the door to get one last glimpse of me before leaving prison. I saw my cousin in the crowd of men at the door in the other building. The clanking of metal from the front door is heard and a guard appears in view.

The officer in the tower opens the door in front of me and as I walk toward the guard waiting to escort me, I ask if I can speak to my cousin at the door in the other building. The guard says yes and I approach the door and offer some encouraging words to my cousin about doing time, seeing and don't see, hearing and don't hear. Walking towards the front door of the building I stopped, turned, and took one last look at the faces peered to the glass door at both buildings looking at me. More metal clanking as the front door opened to let the guard and me out.

The walk began and I really could not fathom what was happening, after a decade locked up. We walked towards the main administration building which could be seen off in the distance. As we approached the gate, I heard it automatically click to unlock. I could hear the guard's walkie-talkie with codes and calls sounding off as this had become a normal part of everyday life for me. We walked approaching another yard, the sound of another gate "click." The gate opened and I'd switch hands carrying my sheet full of stuff because one hand and arm were tiring out.

After walking through three yards, through three gates, and another metal door clanking, we reached the Administrative building. I moved, (by habit) to walk alongside the wall, mainly keeping my head down. Leaving the majority of the hallway walkway open to guards passing by. We Entered another locked metal door area where I was instructed to put my sheet of letters, pictures, and cards on the floor in front of an empty countertop. Then I was ushered and locked into the same cell I was put in upon entering prison 10 years prior.

In the waiting cell, there was nothing but a gray concrete floor, an open exposed metal toilet in the corner, and a brass drain in the center of the floor. There were no seats or benches. There was just flooring. More than two hours had passed when the door popped open and I was called out and looked at the clock on the wall. I knew minutes before the door popped that I would be called due to hearing an all but familiar sound.

Mississippi Department of Corrections

Discharge Certificate

TO WHOM IT MAY CONCERN:

The undersigned, Director of Records of the Department of Corrections of the State of Mississippi, hereby certifies that:

MDOC Number: **T8164**   Name: **Smith, Sidney Harrington III**

SSN		Date of Birth	**02/18/1970**
Race	**Black**	Sex	**Male**
Height	**5'09**	Weight	**200**
Hair	**Black**	Eyes	**Brown**
Complexion	**Medium**	Build	**Medium**
Marks/Scars	**N/A**		
Cause Number(s)	**B2401-97-01141, B2401-97-01142, B2401-96-00454**		

Who was convicted by the Circuit Court of **Harrison** County for **Grand Larceny x2, Transfer of Controlled Substance** and was sentenced to **5,5,20cc** Year(s) in the Mississippi Department of Corrections with **0** Year(s) Suspended, and **20** Year(s) to Serve and **0** Year(s) Post Release Supervision, **0** Year(s) Unsupervised/Non-Reporting Probation.

That, MDOC Number **T8164** Name **Smith, Sidney Harrington III** has completed sentence service of **20** Year(s) in the Mississippi Department of Corrections and is hereby **DISCHARGED ON October 30, 2014** due to Expiration of Sentence.

That, according to law, MDOC Number **N/A** Name **N/A** is hereby remanded to the supervision of the Mississippi Probation and Parole Board to complete the suspended portion of this sentence under the jurisdiction of the court.

Witness my hand and seal, this __15th__ day of __October__, 2014.

Jeworski Mallett
Director of Records

After being locked up for more than 10 years, I'd heard and become very accustomed to the sounds of chains being carried and then dropped on the floor. Any movement and transportation of prisoners came with jewelry (chains). Without sight, you could hear the officer coming because of the chains rustling together. Then, all of a sudden, the sound would stop and all the chains dropped hitting a cement floor at one time. Again, without sight, you can picture what's happening as you hear the noise of chains moving, you know it's the officer bending over separating and untangling the chains. Then you can hear them dropping sets of ankle shackles and waist chains with handcuffs individually on the floor at different equally spaced positions.

Lying on the floor in the cell hearing this I knew that it was almost time. The door popped and I was called out and positioned in front of my jewelry. My legs were spread about shoulder distance apart. A guard locked shackles on my feet and locked a master lock chain around my waist tight as if it was a belt. Both my hands were placed in handcuffs attached to the waist chain. Lastly, the guard would lock the handcuffs in place with a small pin-like key so they would not get any tighter around my wrist.

Grabbing my sheet while hand-cuffed and shackled was a little difficult, but I managed to bounce it off my legs as I walked out to the van. Still, in total shock and disbelief about this whole event, I refused to allow myself to become one with it because I was afraid of the disappointment in being turned around, this whole thing seemed unreal.

I think after spending an entire decade in the prison I was institutionalized, and I had that mentality. I had forgotten the concept of freedom. I had arrived in Hattiesburg, Mississippi, and now was being released from my shackles and handcuffs after the van ride. Driving away from the van in the car with my wife was surreal. As I turned and veered to look back at the guards, I was still in disbelief that this had actually happened. I was thinking, "This can't be real."

Ephesians 3:12

In him and through faith in him we may approach God with freedom and confidence.

Chapter 4

GOD ORDERED MY STEPS

My Last High

My last high started being my last high about three days before it all ended. Let me clarify that last sentence. What I am trying to say is that my last high was a binge where I was continually getting high every day for more than 40 days. The beginning of it being my last high was when the intensity of getting high began to look like a suicide mission with the drugs as well my behaviors.

The cultivation of my last high began around the time of the month I had to report to my parole officer. I had a certain day and time that I was to report to him. That time was approaching, and I tried to stop using so I could pass the random observed drug test. Crack only stays in your system for three days. I could not stop using crack, despite knowing that I would be drug tested and would test positive for illicit substances. I would immediately be arrested and returned to prison. It was as if none of what I just mentioned mattered while getting high.

What makes this whole thing so weird is that it did matter because in the back of my mind I knew exactly what was going to happen. Knowing that I was about to go back to prison only made me get high faster and with more drugs. It was as if time was running out and I could not get high fast enough. So, the last three days started with the clock ticking backward because I was on a schedule to report into the parole office and my appetite for crack was bottomless.

Where did I get the money to fund this three-day, all-in binge on crack? I seemed to have an unquenchable lust for respiratory failure and heart attack due to ingesting enough cocaine to kill 4 elephants. I robbed my house. Yep, no need to reread that last sentence, you read it correctly. I robbed my own house. It started with a phone call outside on my back patio. I argued with my wife about not giving me money for cigarettes. I wanted cigarettes almost like cocaine. I got tired of arguing with her about why she should give me her last two dollars so I could go buy cigarettes.

I went outside on the back patio looking for butts that I had thrown down so I could light up and burn the tips of my fingers. While outside searching the ground for butts to smoke I made a call to the parole office. I asked to speak with my parole officer. When he answered the phone, it was as if he knew I was high. I kind of felt like he had facetime and could see me right then tripping out. I was supposed to report like in two days and I remember him saying these words "Just don't run." Panic hit for me at that moment and went into overdrive. It was too late to stop using for purposes of passing a drug test because of the fact I previously mentioned. "Cocaine stays in your system for at least three days," I told myself. The drug testing panel is immediate with results, and I will be arrested and handcuffed at that moment. The master manipulator went to work right alongside the dope fiend.

First things first. I had two days left and I knew I needed to score big dope to stay high. I called a local thrift store that I had been selling small miscellaneous stuff out of my house. The owner knew me because I would bring different things to his shop every day riding a bike. I called him and told him I was moving and needed to sell everything in the house. I asked him if he had a truck and trailer or a van. We set a time for the thrift store owner to show up the next day when I knew Judy would be at work. He said he would show up at 9:00 am the next day. The thrift store owner knew I had nice stuff because I had sold him brand new men's shoes, Ralph Lauren men's shirts, a bicycle, lawn equipment, and other miscellaneous items.

My Master Plan

The master manipulator went to work on how to stay out of prison. I had just finished securing a large drug deal for myself tomorrow. I thought for a second about how and what I could do to reverse the inevitable. I remembered the name of a volunteer chaplain that visited the prison every month for a decade. He was a white guy named Danny Pierce. This guy would come to prison and talk about Christ, himself, and some rehabilitation center that he opened up. I remembered him continuously saying, "when you get out and need help call me." Well, I had already made that call for help twice.

This guy had taken me into his treatment center not once, but twice within the last 6 months. Both times I went there high and drugged out of my mind, hungry, stinking, and desperately needing rest and sleep. Both times he admitted me into the program and both times I ate, took a shower, put on clean clothes from the treatment center's clothing donation, slept literally for about 4 days, and left the treatment center. I went there both times only for food, a shower to clean up, rest, and then left to go get high again. So, when I contacted him again for the third time Danny Pierce had no reason to take me into treatment again without any money to pay.

I needed a quick respite, looked this guy up, and contacted his drug and alcohol treatment center again. I called, begged, and pleaded with him for one more chance and he finally said ok. I told him about my parole officer and the huge probability of me going back to prison. Danny Pierce agreed to talk with my parole officer and offered me help that I didn't deserve. The whole time I was talking with him and begging him I never once thought about treatment, GOD, or recovery. My mind was set on staying out of prison and that alone.

I agreed to the terms he stated but was not listening or committing to doing anything he was talking about. Once a bed at his treatment center was secured and the date of entry locked in, I started creating this document to present to my parole officer. I typed the document up thinking that it would have a more important, believable look and feel if it was typed. Just more manipulative garbage because I had not considered going into treatment at all. At this point, I was just making up stuff that could get my behind out of a really bad, tight jam.

The document I typed had the name of the treatment center which is Mercy House Ministries. I listed the address and phone numbers. I also included the length of stay that Mercy House Ministries offered, which was a one-year minimum. So, I had conjured up what I thought was the best chance to stay out of prison, which was to commit myself to some rehabilitation center for a year with stipulations that if I left the treatment center before completing my stay, he could send me to prison.

I said to myself that this was a good, documented plan and should work to keep me out of prison. Of course, there were no guarantees. My parole officer's mind could already have been made up to send me back to prison. The truth is I had already violated several of the terms, conditions, and policies of parole as well as breaking laws. If he sent me back to prison, he would have been well within the frames of justice. I settled this issue in my mind that prison was very possible for me within the next two days. I knew I was responsible for this problem and had done more than enough illegal activities to warrant it. I decided not to run from the law and become a wanted fugitive.

I honestly thought the plan that I'd conjured up was pretty good and just might work. Two days later I was due to report to the parole office in Gulfport. This is a place I was very familiar with having been reporting there for more than two years. I was angry at myself for being in the position of going to prison again and I was extremely doubtful that anything could keep me free, including this brilliant crackhead master manipulator plan that I'd come up with while I was high. The more I thought about the moment of going to that parole office the more dope I needed to smoke thinking the high euphoric feeling was counteracting the negative fearful thoughts of going back to prison.

Everything around me began to tighten and tense up with thoughts of going back to prison and/or going into another long-term residential rehabilitation center. With less than 48 hours left on the clock, the only thing I knew to do that in my mind made life easier to deal with, was getting high. The more I thought about going back to prison and the little time that I had left, it was almost as if I was given a death sentence. In my mind, I only had two days left to get high so I needed to go all out with a bang.

I began rummaging through my wife's belongings. I'd been away in prison and didn't know what was in the house. Outside of that, I didn't care. I was only interested in the stuff that I thought the thrift store guy would pay for so I could sell it and use the money to fuel my drug addiction. I went through rooms, drawers, cabinets, and storage areas like an animal. I mean I remember working up a sweat ripping through stuff looking for checks, credit card statements, and bank account information. At this point in my mind, I did not know what a wife was and to me, she was just another person in my way of getting high.

I had no feelings of compassion, love, or concern for any other human beings, including my wife. I wanted to secure the biggest drug high ever because deep inside, I knew it would be my last high for a long time, if not forever. Up all night getting high, and while being high, I dug through stuff looking for anything of value to sell to the thrift store guy the next day so I could keep the high going. All this was going on while Judy was asleep so she could work the next day.

The next day, after I had been up all night with no sleep, my wife got up and was ready to leave for work. "Finally," I thought, "let the games begin." Judy took one look at me and explained that I could not stay in the house while she was at work. I knew that was coming and had already mentally prepared to listen, lie in agreement, and use the comfort of being in the house all day while she was at work to get high. Not only did I know and plan to be in the house, but I'd also decided to re-do yesterday's activities all over again on a larger scale.

While Judy was getting ready for work, taking a shower, or blow-drying her hair, I was getting high and going from room to room unlocking windows for easy re-entry after she had left. She was smart or I would have done this before. Judy was hip to my little schemes because she went behind me checking and relocking each window and door, I had just left open. Of course, I didn't find this out until I was in the backyard waiting for her to drive off. As I began to go from window to window trying to open them, it hit me that she was smart enough to check and made sure they were all locked. Well, that put me in a bind. I had no cigarettes, was running out of dope, and at that moment no way of getting more. Running out of dope can be very frightening, especially with no money or an easy way of obtaining more.

Sitting in the backyard, broke down and desperate, I called the dope dealer. I had no money and he knew it. He had sold thousands of dollars in dope to me. The dope dealer didn't even want to talk to me knowing that I had nothing else to offer him of value. I pleaded with him to give me some dope based upon all the money I'd already spent with him. I made up stuff about money that I was supposed to get and that I would be able to pay him later that day because I knew it was going to be my last high. He hung up on me. I broke a glass pane on the back door. I reached in to unlock the door. I was in a panic. I needed dope and I needed lots of it and quick. Inside the house, the only thing I could do for sure to secure my last high was exactly what I'd done the day before. I made the calls to the thrift store and dope dealer simultaneously.

The thrift store owner wanted an explanation about what I was doing and why my wife called and bought the stuff back last night. I give him an explanation. I told him that it was my house, my stuff, and we were getting a divorce. I explained that he would face no legal issues by purchasing what I offered. The thrift store owner stated that he needed time to get his van. That would take about an hour and he'd be at my house. I told him that I'd be awaiting his arrival. The dope dealer told me to call him when the thrift store owner arrived and I did.

I'm sad to say that nothing in the house was off-limits to be sold. I didn't care about anything except getting as much dope as I could. The thrift store owner walked through the house pointing at furniture, dishes, microwave ovens, electric can openers, stating dollar amounts after each point. I agreed with yes, yep, and constantly held my hand out for money. Room to room this happened. He bought clothes, shoes, jewelry, decorations, and antiques, I sold any and everything for crack.

I scored plenty of dope and got pretty high. I was looking out the windows wondering when the neighbors were gonna catch on to what I was doing and call the police. I spent hours running around the house hiding dope, fixing crack pipes, peeping out of windows, and hitting the pipe. My wife called a couple of times throughout the day to check in with me and I lied to her.

I knew exactly, to the minute, what time she would be home from work. I was not going to be there to witness that. My phone rings and it's her. Judy is screaming and crying, "How could you do this again? What am I going to do?" She wanted to know where I was and if I was safe. She wanted me to come home, and said she would come and get me. All people in my life up to this point had deserted me. I thought she must be crazy because I knew that she was not trying to trick me into coming home for any other reason than she cared. She just wanted me to be okay, safe, and warm. I knew that was it, my last high.

I'd already made a deal with my parole officer and the treatment center in Hurley, MS. I put whatever clothes I had left in garbage bags and had already set them outside the house. I called a couple of people from the NA and AA program asking for help. I needed a ride to the treatment center. I'd arranged for a ride to pick me up and take me to the treatment center in Hurley, MS.

I had drugs with me. I sat outside all night under a blanket finishing off the drugs until they opened the next day. That was the end of the drugs. I was done.

How many times had I ignored God trying to speak to me? How many miracles did I refuse to see? How many times did I refuse the helicopter, the boat, the jeep? God tried time after time to rescue me and never once gave up. God does not give up even when we are on our last leg. This is the story of God's grace and me accepting the grace that had been offered so many times.

My Burning Bus: My Spiritual Event

I briefly discussed this during the introduction, but here are the details of my "Burning Bush moment." My burning bush moment was a significant spiritual event.

Months into my serious attempt to stay sober, I was about to throw it all away. I stood in my dorm room at Mercy House Adult and Teen Challenge, a residential treatment center in Georgetown, Mississippi. Teen Challenge is a drug and alcohol rehabilitation center with more than 2,000 facilities internationally.

The program was faith-based.
I'd cycled in and out of plenty of rehabs during nearly three decades addicted to crack cocaine. None of the other rehabs were like this. We spent all of our time learning about God, Jesus, and the Bible. We worked at an in-house thrift store, an auto repair center, and a craft workshop. Surrendering to God and following Jesus were the keys to sobriety, we were told.

I wasn't sure I believed that. I'd started using crack as a teenager in Oakland, California. I became an addict, a dealer, a thief, and a homeless junkie living behind a dumpster. I was a dad who walked out on his child to get high, a fugitive from the law, and a former inmate in a Mississippi State Penitentiary.

Now I am here. Somehow, I'd convinced my parole officer to go easy on me after I got caught using drugs following my release from prison. I'd conned so many people over the years, including my wife, Judy, who was crushed that not even 13 years behind bars could drive the addiction out of me.

I couldn't use drugs at the Mercy House Teen Challenge. But in my heart and mind, I still had the habits of an addict. I held part of myself back. My main question today was, how can I maneuver my way out of this?

On one particular day, I let my self-control slip and I was mad. I'd been pulled off one job and reassigned to another. I felt disrespected. "I'm sick of this place," I thought. "I want out." At that moment, I didn't care if I wound up in prison. At least there I knew how to get respect.

I snuck into my dorm room where no one would see me. We weren't supposed to be in our rooms during the day. I threw my stuff in a bag. Mercy House wasn't a locked facility. No one could stop me from leaving. I couldn't wait to get high. Might as well go out in style. I paused. There would be no going back if I walked out. I was 42 years old. A prison sentence now might as well be a life sentence. Judy had already filed divorce papers three times then changed her mind because she was a stubbornly hopeful person. This time she'd be gone for good.

"God!" I shouted. "If you are who they say you are here, you need to show up right now and fix this! Because I am done!" I stopped. Not real sure what happened next, I was calm and I stayed.
It would be amazing to be forgiven and start over with a clean slate. Could I really become a man Judy relied on and respected? Could I stop running and live as a godly person? I stood there in my room agonizing over what to do.

"God!" I shouted again.

This time I did hear a noise. Someone sat up in one of the bunks and stared at me. One of my roommates is sleeping off a sick day. How much of my ranting and raving had he heard? He gave me a strange look and slunk out of the room.

I hung my head. God was not coming to my rescue. And again I was calm, as if I were the only person on the planet at that moment. I had no earthly idea what was happening to me, but I knew I was different, changed. Maybe a week later, I finally realized GOD had healed me.

There was no booming voice from on high. No shining light. No big clouds of smoke. Just an inner certainty that God had heard my cry and turned me onto a new path. I was a new creation, and I knew it! I knew I'd never get into another police car, smoke dope, or go to prison again.

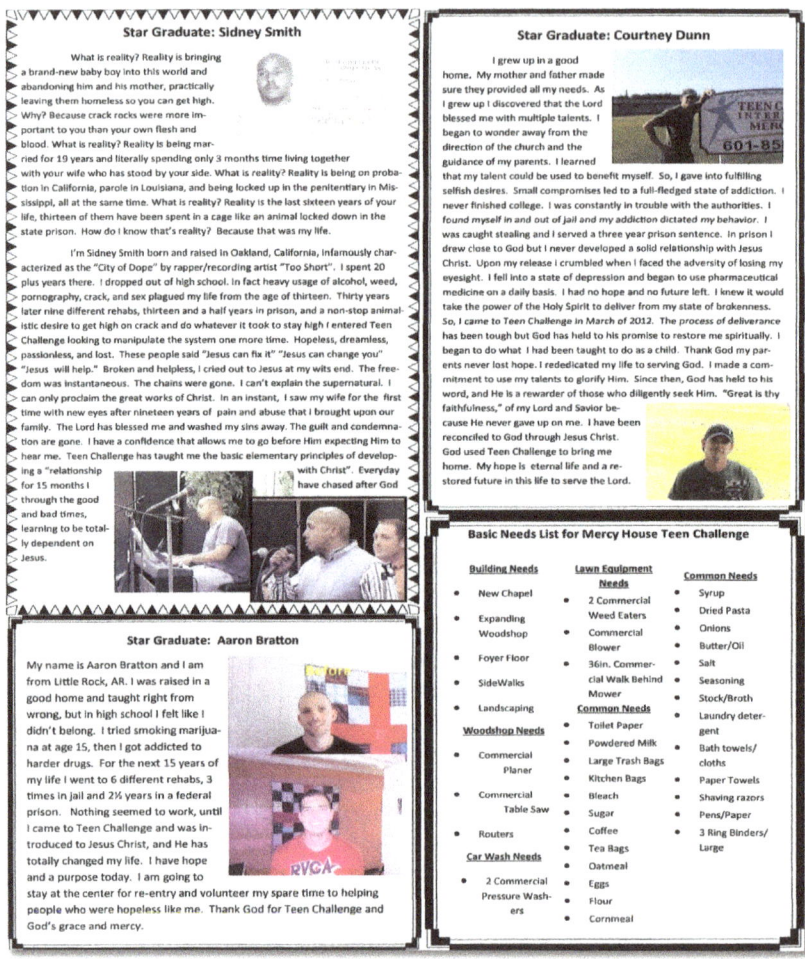

I felt exhausted like I was coming down with the flu. But I knew what I had to do. I unpacked my bag and returned to work. Over the next following days, I struggled to understand what had happened. There was no doubt in my mind I would never use drugs again, or commit a crime, or betray Judy.

But how? It seemed too good to be true that God had simply removed that defect from my brain. I committed myself to the Mercy House Teen Challenge program and began praying for real.

During one of those prayers, I got angry at God for healing me so abruptly.

"If you could do that just by snapping your fingers, why did you let me suffer and inflict pain on myself and other people for 27 years?" I demanded.

God answered. He told me "If I would have answered your prayer when you asked me you would have been thinking you had something to do with it".

The next time Judy visited she teared up before she'd even made her way across the parking lot. She knew with one look GOD had Changed me.

I graduated from Mercy House and began living in a whole new way. All my life, I had never held a job for more than six months, never voted, never paid taxes. Now I enrolled in community college, then the University of Southern Mississippi studying to become a social worker. I wanted to help other people like me.

As I mentioned before, I was assigned to a courthouse internship while pursuing my undergraduate degree. It was the same courtroom where I was tried and sentenced to 20 years for dealing drugs and grand larceny. The D.A. who prosecuted my cases was now the Judge overseeing the courtroom. When she saw me in her courtroom she knew that GOD had to have fixed me. I have never had to say a word about what happened, she just knew. She recognizes me outside the court and once asked if she could give me a hug. This story is one that bears repeating because it is one that you might say was a coincidence. I say it was a miracle that I showed up. The judge got to see this miracle in me.

I give talks to professional organizations about the role of religious faith in addiction recovery and the rehabilitation of drug offenders. I know exactly what rehab clients are going through. Not what each one person is dealing with, but I do know the isolation and the very lowest of the lows that drugs can take a person down to the ground.

One recent client came to me after being released from prison. She was stunned to learn that her social worker had once been incarcerated too. We talked about how hard it is to communicate with loved ones from behind bars. She told me that she and her boyfriend, who was also incarcerated, would call friends at the same house, who then placed their cell phones beside one another on speaker. "You get it," she said. And she opened up to me.

On one wall of my office, I've hung my diplomas, awards, and a framed newspaper clipping showing me with the Chief of the Gulfport Police Department. "New Life," the story is headlined. Beside it on the wall is a framed copy of my prison sentencing document. I try to make sure clients see both of those things.

The ruling emotion of an addict is hopelessness. I want my clients to know that there is always hope, not in emotions but facts and faith. The new life God has given me is being offered to them too. He is waiting for you to reach out, first give up trying to fix you and then reach out.

One encounter with Christ changed everything! Judy and I started fresh but I had a lot to repair, rebuild, and clean up. After all, I did clear out our home right before going to Teen Challenge, twice. I can honestly say amid everything I had gone through with the drugs the first few months of Teen Challenge was a dark time for a different reason, the old man had to die.

I was clean, for the first time I had to truly look in the mirror at myself and find my way through faith to someone I'd never been. This was my time alone with God, a time to give up trying to fix myself. Focusing on GODs word, HE created a new me with a brand-new identity, literally a new creation. HIS story of my life is truly Unbelievably amazing.

> II Corinthians 5:17
>
> *Therefore, if any man be in Christ, he is a new creature; old things have passed away; behold, all things have become new*

Chapter 5

A NEW LIFE

When I enrolled and transferred to the University of Southern Mississippi I applied for admission into the School of Social Work. During the selection process into the School of Social work, I was required to complete three classes and a short internship over the summer semester. My selection into the social work program was dependent on how I did in class, reports from teachers, and the outcome of the internship. This all occurred during my very first semester at the University. The School of Social work did not know about my past at this time. They had no clue I was an ex-convict and past drug addict.

I've always been open about what God has done for me, and my criminal and drug history. However, during this time of my first semester at the University, I was somewhat quiet about my past. I knew I was in a competition of a selection process and there were only a few seats. So, I wanted to focus on my schoolwork and finishing well for the highest selection potential. I did well with the introduction to social work classes. The internship made me worry because it required background checks. I was afraid my past would be exposed, and I would not be allowed to intern nor continue in school at the University. Ye of little faith!

The internship process began towards the end of the summer semester, and it had a huge pool of companies, facilities, agencies, and non-profit organizations. The University had a plethora of internships available to choose from. I was sent to complete my internship at the Harrison County Circuit Drug Court. What does GOD have to do with these steps? The Harrison County Drug Court had a Circuit Court Judge as head of the program and a courtroom assigned to the program. Mind you, this was the same Harrison County Court that previously sentenced me to serve a 20-year prison term. The shocking point of this whole thing is that neither University of Southern Mississppi nor the School of Social Work knew about my criminal or drug history and for me to end up in the same building in the exact same courtroom was Unbelievably Amazing!

The Judge over the Harrison County Drug Court during my internship was, at the time of my sentencing, an assistant district attorney and the prosecuting attorney on many of my cases. Yep, GOD ordered my steps by sending me back into the same courtroom that I had years before been sentenced to serve twenty years in prison, now to complete an internship. The Judge knew exactly who I was when she saw me due to my past terrible criminal history. I would also venture to say at this point, that she also had to have known that GOD had changed my life as she witnessed me in her courtroom with a badge. Now I stand in her courtroom dressed appropriately, in my right mind, and there as an official with a badge, and not as a criminal, must have been mind blowing.

The moment I walked back into the same courtroom felt like a victory for me. It felt like God was leading me all the way. Grace abounds and grace is amazing.

In just a few short months an article was published in a local paper. At first, I was reluctant, but I believed if even one person benefited from reading or hearing about my story, then sharing my story with others was my witness to be shared. This article had the following headline: "A Miracle: Social Work Student Flourishes Following Years of Addiction, Incarceration" This was written by Ellen Cirurczak, of the Hattiesburg American News.

JESUS, WHO HE IS—UNBELIEVABLY AMAZING

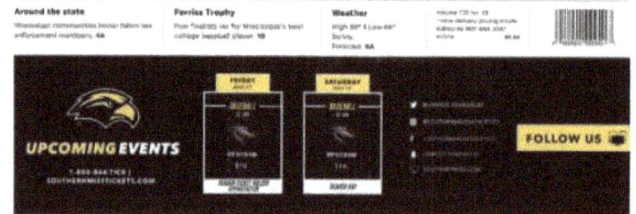

This article retold some of the experiences of my past life on the street and some experiences of prison. Things were brought up that I had not shared openly with others but now the entire community was reading in the paper. I was "outed" so to speak. It felt good to be open and honest about my life and it confirmed what I thought when I accepted the interview. If even one person benefits from the article, then I did the right thing. We are called to plant seeds; to give others a chance to turn and look and to see everyday miracles that happen. Miracles do happen every day. We have to just turn and look and notice the miracles happening around us.

The articles also shined a spotlight on some of the achievements of my undergraduate time at Southern Mississippi and part of the article that was shared about my current life included my "about face." She wanted to show the amazing way my life changed after my time that I spent at Teen Challenge and went to college. It read as follows:

Dr. René Drumm, an associate dean, and Professor of Social Work on the Gulf Park campus remembered being struck by Smith's depth when she interviewed him as a prospective applicant to the Social Work program.

"He was a really interesting person to interview because he is naturally gifted as a speaker. However, at some of the questions when I probed, he stopped to think about them, and think deeply. And that impressed me."

Smith has left an indelible mark during his time at The University of Southern Mississippi:
- President's List 8 semesters
- McNair Scholar
- Honors College
- Social Work Award of Merit, 2017-18
- BSW Club-Gulf Park President, 2017-18
- Undergraduate Social Work Student of the Year, 2018
- Undergraduate Research Prize, second place, 2018

- Magna Cum Laude graduate with Bachelor of Social Work degree, 2018
- Council on Social Work Education Minority Fellowship, 2019

Smith even used his personal experiences as a way to frame his Honors College research project, working with Dr. Drumm as his adviser to study whether religion or spirituality leads to more successful addiction treatment outcomes, as measured by retention and completion rates.

"There's no doubt he will be amazingly successful in his career, just as he was in his career as a student in our program," Drumm says. "He will make a difference for people in how they look at addiction, how they look at overcoming barriers and even over minority issues. He will be able to help people because he's a real advocate on that front as well. He's overcome more obstacles than most of us face in a lifetime. I'm very proud of him."

Karen Aderer, a lecturer in Social Work on the Gulf Park campus, praises Smith's social skills in networking and making a real connection with everyone he meets. She punctuates stories about his prolific fundraising skills with laughter over the absurdity of how much money he raised: $2,000 for a Golden Basket project that provided food, clothing, and other gifts to needy families on the Coast at Thanksgiving; and nearly $1,000 more at the Gulf Park campus' annual Jazz and Blues Festival.

THE UNIVERSITY OF SOUTHERN MISSISSIPPI.

School of Social Work
www.usm.edu/social-work

118 College Drive #5114
Hattiesburg, MS 39406
601.266.4163
Fax 601.266.4167

730 East Beach Boulevard #5128
Long Beach, MS 39560
228.214.3262
Fax 228.214.3272

January 12, 2016

To Whom It May Concern,

I am writing to speak about Sidney Smith's many strengths and to recommend him wholeheartedly. I taught Sidney last semester in my undergraduate Intro to Social Work class. He excelled in this class, but even more importantly, he showed interest, self-reflection, asked great questions and participated in every aspect of the class. As part of their coursework, my students must do 40 hours of volunteer work/observation under a social worker. Sidney spoke passionately and eloquently about his placement at Drug Court, and I noticed the other students were impacted positively by his enthusiasm and self-insight. As a later in life returning student, Sidney brought experience and wisdom to the classroom setting, which is always a joy to a professor.

I had additional interaction with Sidney outside of the classroom from his utilization of office hours. Sidney does not hesitate to ask when he is unsure about something, and shows a desire for excellence in all that he does. In fact, he has received straight A's for his last two semesters at USM. He would have a 4.0 GPA at USM due to this, but he took some classes from 1999-98 at USM that lowered his GPA to a still impressive 3.36. In academia, we know that the best predictor of future academic achievement is most recent achievement; from that standpoint I feel that Sidney will only continue to raise his GPA.

Finally, as Faculty Advisor for the Bachelor of Social Work Club, I was impressed with how Sidney showed up at meetings, volunteered to help, and generally went above and beyond what he said he was going to do. He was one of my core students that I could count on. Due to his relationships with two local churches, Sidney was able to secure very generous cash donations from church fundraisers, which helped us to provide food, clothing and presents to our Head Start families.

Sidney has shown he has been a good ambassador of the scholarships he received previously, and I believe he will continue to put great effort and passion into his schooling. Even more impressively, he is passionate about helping people, and using his life lessons to empower and help others. I recommend him wholeheartedly.

Sincerely,

Karen Aderer, LMSW
Clinical Instructor
University of Southern Mississippi
School of Social Work
730 East Beach Boulevard
Long Beach, MS 39560

"Sidney asked me if he could sell these wooden door decorations that had different University names like you hang on your wall or door and it's for USM or LSU," she says of the festival fundraiser. "He wanted to rent a table and sell the items that were donated from an addiction rehab program where he volunteers. I found out it was $50 to rent the table, so I said, 'Sidney, do you think you can sell more than $50 worth?' And he said, 'Oh, I think so.'

"He ended up selling $850 worth. I went by the table, and every time he was talking people up and they were engaged. And door decorations were flying off the table. He has good people skills, and he will talk to anyone.

"He's one of those people who can talk to a homeless person just as effectively as he could talk to a king or a CEO of an organization. He arranged for the BSW Club to be servers at Feed My Sheep, and I could not believe that everyone who came through the line knew him and he knew them! He remembered names, he knew to ask how their mother was or how their new job had worked out. Sidney remembered minute details that are the sort of things that maybe other people would have said, 'Oh, these are homeless people, poor people.'... Every one of them, he treated them like they were a queen or king. I was so impressed by that and you could tell how well-liked he is."

A Community Doubter

Leonard Papania was not convinced. The first time Gulfport's Chief of Police met Sidney Smith; he wasn't sure he completely believed Smith's story. It was at a gathering of community churches about five years ago, and Smith was selling wooden crosses – fundraising again.

"My interpretation was it was part of his recovery," says Papania, then a 28-year Veteran of Gulfport Police Department and the Chief since 2013. "I am your typical cop and was skeptical of his story – maybe it was just another line to sell something. We talked for a little bit, and I moved on. You hear Sidney tell the story. I didn't buy anything."

They continued to cross paths occasionally, and Papania says he began to pay closer attention because of a family member who was struggling with addiction. "The next time I saw him I was speaking at a recovery center where he worked. We recognized each other again and it gave legitimacy to what I was skeptical about before, and we talked while I was there. Another time, when I was asked to speak at a church, he was up front with us and was actually playing the piano and singing, quite beautifully. At that point, I knew he was for real so I had him tell me his whole story again."

Papania says they were unable to determine if they had previously crossed paths during his time as a narcotics officer and when Smith was an addict. But now they see each other regularly, and Papania considers Sidney a friend.

"When you look at Sidney, he epitomizes everything we demand of those people who are in criminal lifestyles. We always tell everyone to get their life right and nobody has gotten it right better than Sidney. I mean, not only did he pull himself together, but he is now an accomplished academician and very much involved in saving the community he was a part of. His story is the most impressive thing."

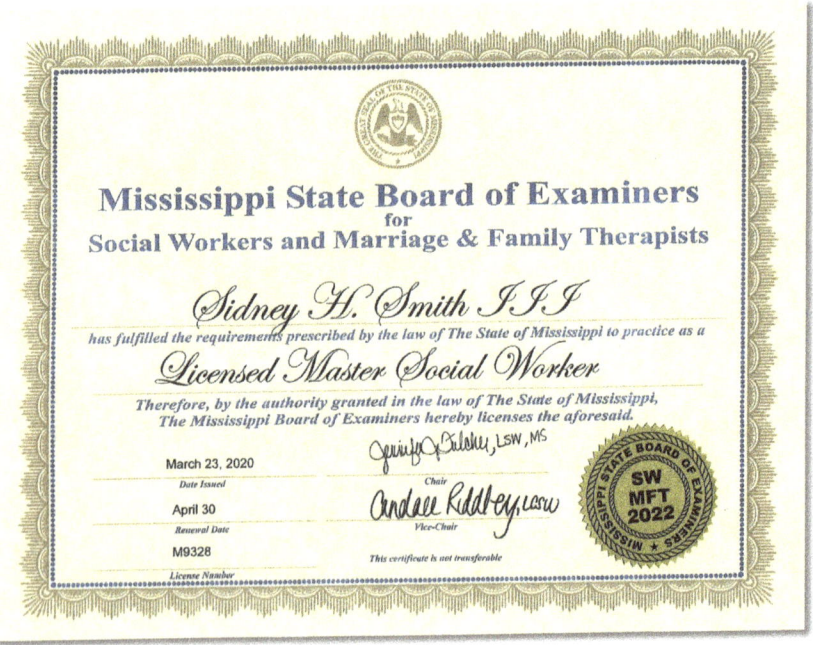

Papania was such an advocate for Smith that he and Smith's former Parole Officer, Agent Steven Gill of the MS Depart. of Corrections, drove to Jackson to support Smith as he was trying to become a Licensed Social Worker by the Mississippi State Board of Examiners of Social Workers and Marriage & Family Therapists.

"He asked me, 'Would you write a letter on my behalf because of my criminal record?'" Papania said. 'I want to go up and testify.' I wore my dress uniform to make an impression on his behalf."

Smith also got in-person support from Ed Blakeslee past president of the board of trustees of the Institutions of Higher Learning, which oversees Mississippi's eight public Universities, as well as Dr. Virginia Adolph, past president of the Mississippi Board of Examiners. It took that extraordinary effort to finally convince the board, which hadn't initially granted Smith's license. "I had done some research to figure out all my crimes are old, 19 to 20 years since I was convicted. I knew everyone knew how God had changed my life. It was a no-brainer for anybody looking at the Dept. of Justice FBI printout versus College transcripts, letters of recommendation, and community support.

- *This has got to be a different person.* I thought the board would be able to see that, but they didn't.

"I understand now they have a responsibility to protect the public and make sure I'm not going to go out with a license and cause harm from things in my past. It's a realistic, very serious concern. They never disclosed to me exactly why, though."

In the end, Smith both passed the licensure exam *and* addressed the board's concerns. He received confirmation last September when he called Billy Dilworth of the State Board.

"I asked if they had made a decision and he said, 'Yes, hold on.' It seemed like I was on hold an eternity, but it was probably 40 seconds. He came back and said they had approved my licensure. I got emotional, yes, I bowed beforehe LORD, YES!

"I doubted, I stressed. I knew that I wanted it because it would help to calm a lot of what was going on inside me as far as a career in Social Work. I could just rest and go forward without having to worry about that as an added weight."

I knew God had me in loving arms but I was trying to guide my own steps. Once again, I was taking back over when I knew God had more grace for me.

A NEW LIFE

My confirmation for a two-semester internship at the VA dragged out until right before I needed it for the Fall of 2018. I eventually got a letter and a badge from the Federal Government with a May 2019 expiration date, which took me through that Spring.

"The only thing not at the VA is kids," Smith says of the services. "There's medical, psych wards, gerontology, dementia, short term, blind rehabilitation, substance abuse, ICU, and acute. If you can't find a passion there, you haven't got one. One of the things that excited me about the opportunity to go there was something Ms. Aderer shared with us about how more Veterans come home and commit suicide than are casualties of war, 22 per day. You can make a difference there."

By his own account, Sidney didn't have any scars, physical or psychological trauma from his years as an addict. "I don't recall anything traumatic that lasted as a result of what I've been through in my life. What I've been told and what I know to be true is that every Social Worker needs a Social Worker. When I need help, I will periodically seek out counseling from friends and other Social Workers about different issues. As far as being traumatized or needing medication or continuous intervention or help, no, I haven't come to that bridge."

As stated before, I have a son from a previous relationship. This is the son I abandoned at birth and who came to visit me in prison with all those quarters. Now Jordan Jamal Lion is in his twenties and graduated in May of 2019 from the University of Central Florida, he allowed me to be presen a witness his graduation.He actually called me Dad once and I am so proud of him. I never did anything for him, his mother did an outstanding job as a single parent. I sat there for 13 years of his life in a penitentiary, and he had every reason to be angry and hate me. But he tells me he loves me. I left him and his mother practically homeless so I could get high. Crack was more important to me than my flesh and blood.

I also am close to my own mother now. Her name is Gloria Mills and I want to lift her up on the pages of my book. My mom moved to Mississippi to help take care of Jordan when I went to prison. I know she had a rough time watching me spiral all the way down like I did.

I even stay in touch with my old Parole Officer Agent Gill. Agent Gill considers me more like a co-worker now, I believe.

"It's a very rare, very uncommon occurrence to stay in touch after the fact," Agent Gill says. "He has kept me up-to-date on his progress, his education. You always want to hear good things are happening with somebody. I've invited him to speak at functions we've had and classes we teach with MDOC. He provides inspiration and motivation to people who are going through a similar situation to what he's been through.

"I guess what stands out the best is that he didn't come out and carry that institutionalized mentality that you fear for those who have spent several years in prison. I didn't witness him having that. He's been able to come out, gain employment, go back to family life and prosper. I don't want to say it's unusual, but it's not necessarily expected. The thing I recognize and appreciate about him is that he doesn't let obstacles get in his way and hold him back. He finds ways over, under, or around. It's inspiring."

I can look back to a time not long ago, when I was still an addict and couldn't envision a scenario where I would find my way out, much less flourish as I have. However, now when I do look back, it's like I was in another universe. At the time I had no idea that God was right there. I just needed to turn and look. Those Christians who invited me to eat and allowed me to clean up, they were a lifeboat to save me. I took them as some people who were not very bright. They were kind of funny, even.

Now, the biggest thing I want my story to do is to give people hope. The lifeline is there for each person to accept. Because of what I've learned about Social Work and substance abuse, there is a void of

A NEW LIFE

hope. Drug abuse is rampant in our society. I'd go so far as to say every family in America has been affected one way or another by legal or illegal abuse of drugs.

For someone to provide a way of escape gives hope, an immediate infusion of hope, like an injection. That's the basis for me. It's a drug for me, to be able to look someone else in the face and speak to their desperation, to know where they are and what they're feeling at that moment. And to gather it up and say, 'It doesn't have to be that way.

> Romans 15:13
>
> *May the God of hope fill you with all joy and peace as you trust in Him, so that you may overflow with hope by the power of the Holy Spirit.*

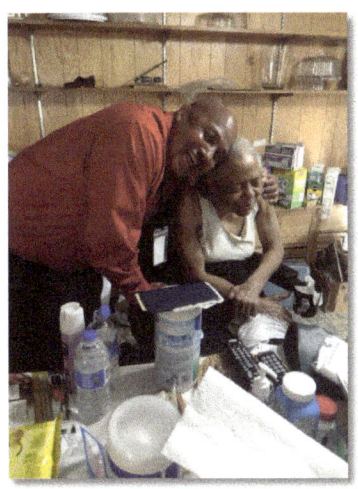

Chapter 6

MOVING FORWARD

My life has been transformed from one extreme to the other. College was a good place for me because I love learning. In my undergraduate and graduate studies, I seemed to fit right in because of my thirst for information. The topics were relevant and the subject matter was the means to the path that I was on to serve God and the people who were put in my path.

I am a member of Phi Alpha, Phi Theta Kappa, PSI CHI, and Alpha Kappa Mu honor societies. I was President of the Bachelor of Social Work Club (BSW Club) and was a member of the Afro-American Student Organization (AASO). That allowed me to be further involved in activities benefiting the community and campus. As an Honors College student, I wrote a Thesis titled *Addiction Treatment Outcomes and Spirituality*. What is the Relationship?

I was then awarded the McNair Scholarship. This helped prepare me for the application process to graduate school. Duing school, I became a full-time employee of Gulf Coast Mental Health Center, Crossroads Recovery Treatment Center, a residential treatment center where I was twice a resident who was kicked out for unruly behavior. I am working around and for Social Workers.

Now I am a Social Worker who works with others. I will be working my new job and starting a non-profit called Right Turns Christian Counseling Center by the time this book is published. The IRS has awarded me 501 3 c status to create a local faith-based treatment center. I have my Bachelor's and Master's degree with License in Mississippi and Alabama.

> James 5:15-16
>
> *And the prayer offered in faith will make the sick person well; the Lord will raise them up. If they have sinned, they will be forgiven. Therefore, confess your sins to each other and pray for each other so that you may be healed. The prayer of a righteous person is powerful and effective.*

A Lonely Soul

I try to wear my faith on my sleeve. I want others to know what God has done for me because then they will know if God can perform miracles in my life than surely that can happen in their life as well. I had a very sad conversation with an older gentleman on the phone last week. He was so depressed. He needed to have a difficult conversation with someone but did not know if he could deal with the pain of how the conversation might go.

One of the things he said was that he had done some bad things in life and he felt like he just could not come back from all of the things in his past. Now I wish I had this book published by the time this conversation had taken place because he could have read about my story and hopefully benefited. If I can come back and live in God's glory and peace, surely this man could too!

Talking to this man taught me an important lesson. It's about a person's perspective of how far down they have gone. To this man, he went all the way down too far to get back up. He knew he had done so many good things, but he still felt his bad outweighed the good. The problem being he had not thrown himself on the prison floor so to speak and wailed to God. Sometimes we have to let it all go and just accept grace as it is offered.

I told my friend, "When you are ready. When you are tired enough to stop trying on your own to measure the good against the bad, God will be waiting for you. It's about grace. No one can earn it. No one can be good enough. Not me and not you. We just have to turn toward God and accept the gift."

He agreed with me, but he still has to find out for himself. Oh how I wish he would.

God's Grace

What is this gift of grace? For me it was relief from addiction to drugs. For someone else, it could mean any number of things. For this friend I was talking to, It is probably going to mean facing some things he may not want to own, owning them and then being able to finally move on. Jesus had a timely way of meeting a variety of people in the Scriptures. For different people he spoke to their needs at that time. What he said to Zacchias, he did not say to Peter. He had a different message for Peter. He also had a different message for the woman at the well, who Jesus wasn't even supposed to talk to in public in that day and time. And to each person there was God's grace. God sent His Son to teach us how to live different thugh the free gift of eternal life. Jesus turned the world at the time upside down. If we are to live like Jesus, we are called to be in the world but not of the world. What does that even mean? Here we are in the world. Or on planet Earth. But we do not have to partake in the very things that destroy God's creation a defy HIS word. The things of the world are power, greed, guilt, envy, and shame. Those are the things that serve to take you further from God when you are in the world because those are the things that are of the world. Those things do not come from God.

Grace is from God. Love, charity, peace, kindness, honesty, honor, and gratitude come from God. You can tell the difference if you start to go down the road that is not from God because those things just further separate you from who you were created to be and to serve. But once you turn away and accept God's grace then it is like seeing the light coming to shine through. Everything comes out in a brighter way. Does this mean everything is always easy? Of course not. But in the midst of any sadness or hard difficulties, you know God walks beside you.

I feel like everyone I have encountered has been a messenger of God's grace. I know there is a lot of talk about Black Lives Matter and there are so many lines that divide us. I think to myself, "Here I am a man of color and yet, I have had so many Caucasian men and women who have supported me and lifted me up. I know it isn't always the case for many of my Black brothers and sisters, but I think if we could all just find the common ground of what brings us together more than what divides us, the entire world would be a better place.

Coming to God and looking up instead of looking down is how my story began. As long as I was looking down into the trash cans, I could not see the people who were there to help me. When I was face planted and passed out, I could not look up to see who God had sent to bring me grace. You cannot find what you are looking for in a bottle, a needle, gambling, sex, or violence. God is in those around us who are trying to lift us up. God is here for all of us so we might lift each other up for His Glory.

Nehemiah 8:10

Do not grieve, for the joy of the Lord is your strength.

Chapter 7

RECENT INTERVIEWS

I decided that toward the end of my book, I would let a third party interview some key people mentioned previously in this book. They haven't been discussed recently but were critical throughout my turning point and the following months and years after that.

July 21, 2015

Dear Ms. Wilson:

I am pleased to submit this letter of recommendation on behalf of Sidney Smith. I have had the distinct pleasure of meeting and teaching Sidney this past year at Mississippi Gulf Coast Community College. A driven and enthusiastic learner, Sidney sets high standards and goals for himself while maintaining an outstanding work ethic. In his time at MGCCC, he has maintained a 3.9 GPA, been inducted into the Phi Theta Kappa Honor Society, and graduated with special honors.

Sidney selflessly volunteers his time in the community working with those less fortunate through programs such as Homes of Grace, Teen Challenge, Mercy House Ministries, and Feed My Sheep. Sidney has dedicated his life, including his educational pursuits, to helping those struggling with addiction to transform their lives. When he speaks so joyfully about his work and his goals in life, it is obvious that he has found his calling.

I sincerely believe that Sidney possesses the leadership skills, enthusiasm, and dedication that will make him an excellent addition to your staff, and I recommend him with great confidence. If you need further information, please do not hesitate to contact me.

Sincerely,

Tracey Gillespie
Tracey Gillespie
Mathematics Instructor, MGCCC
(228) 860-0632

"I met Sidney during a learning lab setting," stated **Tracey Gillespie**, College Math Professor, "He came in everyday of three consecutive semesters for tutoring." Tracey Gillespie was one person who was amazed at the impact Sidney had on her while Sidney was just in the class to learn algebra and do the best he could to get through college.

"The impact Sidney had on me surprised me in that I don't judge people. You have no idea what a person has gone through by looking at a person. Not that he kept it from me. He was just there to learn, and we didn't get into specifics right away. When he later said that he lived like an animal or he was an animal, I could *never* see Sidney that way. Sidney religiously impacted me because I could see what he was doing for God.

"At that time in my life I was searching, and I was led to the church I belong to right now. I had suffered losses and Sidney helped me find a church home that he was planting. I realize now why I say, 'I don't know who I am sitting next to and in my work every student has a unique situation.' There isn't anything Sidney cannot achieve."

JESUS, WHO HE IS—UNBELIEVABLY AMAZING

GULFPORT POLICE DEPARTMENT

OFFICE OF THE CHIEF OF POLICE

MAYOR COUNCIL FORM OF GOVERNMENT
2220 15TH STREET
P.O. DRAWER "S"
GULFPORT, MISSISSIPPI 39501
228.868.5959

Billy Hewes
MAYOR

Leonard Papania
CHIEF OF POLICE

October 11, 2017

Mr. Billy Dilworth
Executive Director
MS. State Board of Examiners
for Social Workers and Marriage & Family Therapists

Mr. Spencer Blalock
LCSW
Chair of the Social Work Discipline Specific Committee

Ms. Victoria Murdy
LCSW
Board Member

To All Parties,

    I was contacted by Sidney Smith this date at which time he requested my consideration for a recommendation in advancement in his career path in social work. I was excited to here of his continued successes and more importantly his intention to go further.

    I will say I first met Sidney during a community event where he was selling crosses for a fund raiser. We spoke and he shared his story. In my line of work I hear many stories. I am skeptical by trade, but knew our encounter was by chance and he had nothing to gain in telling me. Over the next few years we have several contacts to include when I was speaking at a local recovery center where he worked. Each time we spoke I began to realize that he was sincere in his recollection of life and his intentions to move forward; he is truly a man driven by faith and love. I have often pondered if during my years as a narcotics detective did we ever come into contact.

    I have been in law enforcement since 1991. For many years I served in the investigation of violations of our drug laws. I have served as Chief of Police for the City of Gulfport for four and a half years. In these years of service I have had the opportunity to fully understand the damaging effects of drug addiction and mental illness. Sadly, I have had the opportunity to

The Chief of Police, Leonard Papania, was also talked to again by a 3rd person. He was already mentioned once in this book, but I thought it would be fun to get his thoughts from someone who had never met him.

"When I met Sidney, I was at a gathering of churches coming together, and this guy was selling wooden crosses. So, I go over and talk to him. I thought he was another guy with a challenging story and a lot of blah, blah, blah. I honestly was a skeptic.

"I attended this event for a 30-Day Treatment Program, and who was the guest speaker? It was Sidney. He talked about the role of responsibility and leadership. He spoke about how vital engagement was for the people of the community. These were not the words of a cross-selling fly-by-night guy. I began to appreciate Sidney.

---

realize how our state and federal governments fail to truly understand and fund the treatment of mental disease and addiction. I have experienced addiction in my own family. So I think I speak with some level of understanding from a professional and personal level.

Sober addicts in recovery are, in my opinion, such an important asset and resource for the mental health and addiction treatment community. Sober addicts with formal education in the field are a must.

I guess you are faced with making two decisions concerning Sidney. First, has he fulfilled all the academic requirements for the position being considered? This only you can measure. The second, and more importantly, will his criminal past lead to an ill effect on his areas of responsibility if he is allow to proceed? I strongly suggest that consideration be made especially when looking at not just how long he has been sober, but what has he done with his life while sober. I recently told Sidney that he is so much more impressive than what "heroes" our nation and media try to portray. Most kids growing up think professional athletes are heroes. I think a man that was addicted to crack cocaine, ate out of dumpsters, served time in prison, and overcame it all and asked me for a letter of recommendation is truly what a hero is.

I am available by telephone, office - 228-868-5964 or cellular telephone - 228-596-8089. I can also appear in person if needed. Thank you so much for the work that you all do and the consideration you are giving to Sydney.

Respectfully,

Leonard J. Papania
Chief of Police
City of Gulfport

"Then I attended an event that coincided with the killing of the police officers in Dallas, and where was Sidney? He was at the piano singing his heart out! So, I gave that man a chance and got to know him. I realized he was truly an accomplished man from where he was to where he is now.

"When it was time for Sidney to get accepted for Social Work by the Mississippi State Board of Examiners of Social Workers and Marriage & Family Therapists, he asked me to write

a letter of recommendation. I turned down writing that letter and instead went in person along with Dr. Virginia Adolf and others to testify in person how much Sidney was impacting the community and our lives as well.

"My feelings are: 'Many times in life you say to someone who has had a criminal past, you need to get your life together. All you need to do is give this man a fair shake so he can give back!'

"We go out to eat from time to time because we are friends now, and I say to him, "I eat fast from days on patrol."

"Sidney says to me, "I eat fast from days in prison."

"People have more commonalities than there are differences."

Agent Steven Gill, Sidney's parole officer, also had nothing but praise about Sidney. Now, Officer Gill had seen some ups and downs, but through it, all, also saw Sidney's shining light.

"When Sidney came out on parole after graduating from the drug and alcohol faith based Adult and Teen Challenge Program, it was different, everything had changed, and Sidney was a new creation. I could see Sidney was different. He was motivated. He was the "perfect Parolee." Sidney always brought in receipts. He had hurdles to tackle, but he did tackle them and kept moving forward. When he faced that last hurdle of substance abuse, and he overcame that, it goes to show, 'where you've been, don't let that define you.' "You can shape your life. Sidney gives back to people going through what he went through and influences individuals who are going through low times. You can stumble, but you can come back up. I can be more, and I can do this. There isn't a roadblock unless you let there be a roadblock.

"Sidney has impacted my life because he has taken it all, and he gives back. He goes further and reminds me of that." **Ted Hearn** is a retired Brigadier General who crossed paths with Sidney right after Sidney left Teen Challenge. He begins his story:

March 7, 2015

Dear Sir,

I am submitting this Letter of Recommendation for Sidney Smith who is seeking available scholarships to continue his college education.

I am a 20 year member of the Board for Feed My Sheep, a soup kitchen in Gulfport, Ms. I met Sidney in early summer of 2013 when he spoke to me about needing a job. Feed My Sheep had no job openings at that time. I became interested in learning more about Sidney. He had led a life of drug addiction and prison time but he had just completed a one year program with Teen Challenge. God and this program had changed his life. I soon discovered that he was blessed with the ability to play the keyboard and sing, especially religious music. He is a born again Christian who uses his music to worship God and he shares it and his testimony with churches and recovery facilities throughout the area. Feed My Sheep hired Sidney in August 2013. He operates a route to pick up day old food items from grocery stores, pastry shops and pizza stores five days each week. It is a part time job, 4 hours per day. Sidney is a happy, friendly and very smart man who is goal oriented. He could have taken a much better paying, full time job, but he wanted to begin college full time to become a social worker. Sidney initiated an annual program to honor and thank all the stores that provide food items to Feed My Sheep. He is a valuable employee and a man of God.

Sidney and I have become close personal friends along with his wife. I am involved daily in the lives of the homeless and the facilities who help them. Sidney is always available to share his music and testimony and try to make a difference in lives that seem hopeless. I have been impressed with Sidney's dedication to his education and desire to excel. He works hard at doing his very best. I am impressed with his commitment and desire to use his education to serve others.

It is my pleasure to strongly recommend Sidney Smith for any available scholarships. He is trying to balance between supporting his family and his education dream that will allow him to help others. Please contact me at 228-861-9017 for more information.

Sincerely,

Thomas R. Hearn Jr.

Thomas R. Hearn Jr, Brigadier General U.S. Army (Retired)

"A dream came to me to get out from behind the counter and get back into serving others, and Sidney was part of that dream when he walked through our doors. In 2013, Sidney came into Feed my Sheep looking for a job. I said we didn't have a job. Then he went down to Trinity Methodist. Sidney and Judy were married there. They didn't have a job available there either.

"Then Sidney asked if he could play their piano. So, they said that he could. So, Sidney began playing and singing on their piano. One by one, the staff showed up to listen and enjoy Sidney's music. Then, they asked Sidney if he would please play in church on Sunday at service. So, I go to service on Sunday, and there is Sidney on the piano!

"It was spiritual and unique. After that experience, it wasn't long before we began a program where we would get day-old items, and we would need a driver to go get those items. So, of course, I offered Sidney the job. He started the route to pick up all the food, which mainly was day-old bread. Sidney developed the route, and it was his first part-time job. Sidney then began his education, and he would work from 7 -12 and then go to school.

For a guy who had been in prison, he had been there, and he had seen it. It took almost all his time to get his associate's degree, then get his Bachelor's degree. Unfortunately, we lost Sidney as an employee because he began school full time. He graduated with the highest honors as Magna Cum Laude and got a Federal Scholarship. He was one out of forty-two people. 'Sidney is a person who utilizes his all to become his all.' We have never been able to replace Sidney."

Finally, last but certainly not least, Pastor Anthony McCullum gave his account about Sidney. He calls Sidney an incredible, talented young man and the best fishing companion he has ever had!

"I realized that my work in the correction institute is not in vain. You don't know what you might accomplish by going there to the prison. Because of Sidney, I know I can still do things to bring about good. Sidney is incredibly influential to everyone he encounters, both professionally and personally.

"He was only married for three months to Judy and then went to prison. When he got out, he had a whole lot of trials and tribulations, and he and Judy went through so much. Judy stuck with him and was so highly supportive. And now Sidney is a Social Worker himself. To me, it is a miracle. He worked so hard to deserve these opportunities, and I am so proud of Sidney. He deserves all good things."

One theme that ran through every conversation is that Sidney has made a lasting impression with each person on this list. Not only is he authentic, but he is also someone who impacts everyone he contacts. I, too, have talked with Sidney, and I have to say, he is the real deal. I am just amazed by his spirit and by his love for God and for life. His devotion to Judy is now so apparent in his words and deeds. I am Sidney's editor and am helping with just a few final edits on his book. It has been an honor to have been chosen by Sidney to do this work. I feel like God set this partnership in motion.

I personally cried when I heard the many people tell their stories and heard Sidney tell his story. It's just incredible how far down Sidney went and then the fantastic journey he followed to come back up. And the patience and steadfastness of Judy. I have nothing but praise for Judy. To have a steadfast partner in life like that is a true blessing. Sidney reflects the Grace of God. That is the true story here. Of course, Sidney had to put forth all the effort; just like Noah had to build the ark, Sidney had to do the work to go to college, do acts of service, and become who he is today. But Sidney will tell you, all his blessings are from the Grace of God. Amen to the hard work and to the lasting friendships Sidney has made.

Matthew 5:16

In the same way, let your light shine before others, so that[a] they may see your good works and give glory to your Father who is in heaven.

Chapter 8

MY MANY BLESSINGS

I have been blessed in many ways. Over the years I have made so many friends and received blessings everywhere I've been. Since I have given over my life to God, doors have been opened and Grace has been abundant. Remember, it is always there to accept. We just have to turn our heads and see what is in store for us!

May 2019, Master of Social Work

The University of Southern Mississippi, Hattiesburg, MS

SAMHSA/Counsel of Social Work Education Minority Fellowship

May 2018, Honors College, McNair Scholar, Bachelor of Social Work, minor in Psychology, The University of Southern Mississippi, Long Beach, MS

Thesis: Addiction Treatment Outcomes and Spirituality: What is the Relationship?

May 2015, A. A. General Studies, Mississippi Gulf Coast Community College, Jefferson Davis Campus, Gulfport, MS

Professional Memberships:

- Council of Social Work Education MFP member (2018-present)
- National Association of Social Workers (NASW 2017-present)
- North American Christian Social Workers (2017 -present)
- MGCCC Alumni (2015-present)

Research Interests:

- Religiosity/Spirituality
- Faith-based drug and alcohol treatment,
- Drug and Alcohol intervention, rehabilitation and prevention
- Evidence based addiction treatment outcomes
- Harm Reduction

Publications:

Smith III, Sidney Harrington, "Addiction Treatment Outcomes and Religiosity: What is the Relationship?" (2018). Honors Theses. 595. https://aquila.usm.edu/honors_theses/595

Training:

- Teen Challenge 14-month Christian Discipleship Program
- CPI Nonviolent Crisis Intervention training program
- CPR certification
- Collaborative Institutional Training Initiative

Service Activities:

Community Service Related to Profession

- Gulfport Police Department Advisory Board Member (2019 – 2020)
- Panelist for the NAACP Promises Unmet. A discussion about mass incarceration and the war on drugs
- Harrison County Drug Court Internship (2015- 2016)
- Home of Grace Drug and Alcohol Rehabilitation volunteer (2013- present)
- Feed My Sheep local soup kitchen (2015- 2019)
- Teen Challenge speaking engagement at a Drug and Alcohol banquet Madison, Mississippi (2014 & 2015)
- Professional Oral Presentation, Addiction Treatment Outcomes and Spirituality. What is the relationship? 26th Annual National Ronald E. McNair Conference Graduate School Recruitment Fair Chicago, Illinois (Oct. 2017)
- Professional Presentation, CE approved panel, Criminal Justice System, University of Southern Mississippi Fall Colloquium (Dec.2017)
- Professional Presentation, Undergraduate Symposium for Research and Creative Activity, University of Southern Mississippi, Honors College April 21, 2018
- Professional Presentation, Addiction Treatment Outcomes and Spirituality. What is the relationship? 47th Annual Alabama-Mississippi Social Work Education Conference, University of Alabama, Tuscaloosa, Alabama (Oct. 25-26, 2018)
- Poster Presentation, Are age, education and religiosity associated with completion of the faith-based Teen Challenge program? National Association of Social Workers Elevate Conference, Natchez, MS, (March 09, 2019)

- Professional Oral Presentation, Addiction Treatment Outcomes and Spirituality. What is the relationship? 2019 Susan A. Siltanen Graduate Research Symposium, The University of Southern Mississippi Graduate School, Hattiesburg, MS (April 11, 2019

Service to the University

- University of Southern Mississippi Student of the Year 2018
- President of the Bachelor of Social Work Club
- Bachelor of Social Work Club Member elected class representative (2016)
- Bachelor of Social Work Club Member (2015-present)
- Coordinator of fundraising event at the USM Annual Blues and Jazz Fest, raising over $800.00

Awards and Honors:

- 2019 Susan A. Siltanen Graduate Research Symposium 2nd place Empirical Oral Research Presentation winner
- NASW Graduate Student 1st place Empirical Research Poster (2019)
- Council on Social Work Education Masters Minority Fellowship 2018-2019
- NASW & The University of Southern Mississippi Social Work Student of the Year Award, (2018)
- Honors College Undergraduate Symposium on Research 2nd place 2018
- The University of Southern Mississippi Hall of Fame Who's Who Award 2018
- Award of Merit, The University of Southern Mississippi 2018
- President of BSW club recognition award (2017)

- Afro-American Student Organization Award of Excellence Recipient (2016)
- Psi Chi National Honor Society (2015)
- Phi Theta Kappa Honor Society (2013)
- Alpha Kappa Mu Honor Society (2016)
- Phi Alpha Honor Society (2017)
- USM Honors College Student (2016-2018)
- Award of Recognition for Service in Leadership and Dedication (2017)

> Philippians 4:13
>
> *"I can do all things through Christ who strengthens me."*

gofundme

Show your support by going to this link
GoFundMe.com/wpz36pw

As a non-traditional student it was a must for me to work a job during my college tenure. When I started in college working on an associate degree I worked for a local Soup kitchen called Feed My Sheep. My schooling and work hours blended well. After school and work daily I began to wash windows for a few local businesses to cover bills, textbooks, and other needed school supplies. My wife, four dogs and I lived very frugally, we didn't have much. A couple from our church gave us their old car so I could get to school and work. I washed windows for local businesses for at least a year. More and more businesses allowed me to wash their windows. I did a good job, and the business owners really liked me. Whenever I pitched a job and gave an estimate, I always informed them about being a late in life college student. I think my story of being a non-traditional college student trying to work extra to offset home and school expenses helped. I don't have any evidence to support that theory, GOD and business owners know.

My wife came up with the idea of a GoFundMe account. She presented it to me, and we agreed to try it. She created the account, named it and posted it to the website. Some people were friends, but most were strangers and or donated anonymously to our college fund. It was completely amazing and a blessing to our family. The GoFundMe account stayed active for about two years and grossed more than $12,000. If you donated to this account, first, thank you again, and second you did a good thing because GOD used your help to accomplish HIS work in my life. Unbelievably Amazing Thanks.

> Thessalonians 5:11
>
> *"Therefore encourage one another and build each other up, just as in fact you are doing."*

CONCLUSION

There isn't a way to conclude this book because this story isn't finished. Just like every life, the story just keeps on going. Ted Hearn talks about being 89 and still finding work to do for the Lord. Our stories go on if we have a breath within our bodies. I just know that every morning I am grateful to see a new day when I wake up! The past only serves to help me know I can help others to not give up when they are down.

God is with us waiting for us to choose to follow him. To ask for help and then start fresh with a new creation in Christ Jesus. God will use you if you accept His grace. It's always there. Just turn and look. You will see your burning bush.

> John 16:33
>
> *"I have told you these things, so that in me you may have peace. In this world you will have trouble. But take heart! I have overcome the world."*

I want to thank everyone who has helped me on my journey

www.ingramcontent.com/pod-product-compliance
Ingram Content Group UK Ltd.
Pitfield, Milton Keynes, MK11 3LW, UK
UKHW020245240426
12048UKWH00026B/1624